Tunisian
Stitch

LEISURE ARTS, INC. • Little Rock, Arkansas

EDITORIAL STAFF

Vice President of Editorial:
Susan White Sullivan

Special Projects Director: Susan Frantz Wiles

Director of E-Commerce and
Prepress Services: Mark Hawkins

Creative Art Director: Katherine Laughlin

Technical Editors: Sarah J. Green and
Cathy Hardy

Technical Writer: Lois J. Long

Editorial Writer: Susan McManus Johnson

Art Category Manager: Lora Puls

Graphic Artist: Becca Snider Tally

Imaging Technician: Stephanie Johnson

Prepress Technician: Janie Marie Wright

Contributing Photographer: Ken West

Contributing Photo Stylist: Sondra Daniel

Manager of E-Commerce: Robert Young

BUSINESS STAFF

President and Chief Executive Officer:
Rick Barton

Vice President of Finance:
Laticia Mull Dittrich

Director of Corporate Planning: Anne Martin

National Sales Director: Martha Adams

Information Technology Director:
Brian Roden

Controller: Francis Caple

Vice President of Operations: Jim Dittrich

Retail Customer Service Manager:
Stan Raynor

Vice President of Purchasing: Fred F. Pruss

**We would like to thank Cascade Yarns for
providing the yarn for this book.
Visit http://www.cascadeyarns.com to see
all of their yarns.**

Library of Congress Control Number: 2013931896

ISBN-13: 9781464707391

Table of Contents

KIM GUZMAN

fills each day with creativity. Whether she's knitting or crocheting a new design or working on a new canning experiment with the fruit and vegetables she grows at her home in Arkansas, she fulfills a lifelong dream—endless creative ventures in a lovely country setting with her family close at hand. Her mother likes to call Kim the garden paparazzi when she rushes out to take photos of flowers, fruit, vegetables, and beautiful butterflies.

The design work that helps Kim realize this dream has won several awards, including eight "Flamies" from the Crochet Liberation Front. One of these was the 2011 award for Best Teacher. Kim has authored several pattern books, and her designs have appeared in yarn craft magazines.

Kim says, "My goal is to produce crocheted items which more closely resemble knitted garments. Even my ribbed garments are designed to specifically avoid bulkiness."

See more of Kim's creations at
KimaneDesigns.net and CrochetKim.com.
She maintains a blog called WIPs 'N Chains at
KimGuzman.wordpress.com
and is an active member of Ravelry.com.

Learn more about Tunisian Crochet in these Leisure Arts books!

Ultimate Beginner's Guide to Tunisian Crochet • # 5599

If you like the ease of working with a crochet hook, but admire the look and feel of knitted fabric, you'll love learning Tunisian Crochet. Award-winning teacher Kim Guzman walks you through the basics and takes you through each step with clear photos and friendly instructions. Nine fresh projects, including the unique Hoodie Vest on the cover, will help you develop the skills you need.

Short Row Tunisian Fashion • # 5729

In less time than you might imagine, you can make fun hats, a scarf, a lacy wrap, a feminine cardigan, and a romantic two-piece cape—all with the "fun and addictive" Short Row Tunisian Crochet technique. Kim says, "Because your rows are constantly changing, it doesn't get monotonous and projects seem to fly off the hook in no time at all."

Chapter 1

An introduction to 14 fundamental stitches of
Tunisian Crochet and their symbols, with full
explanations of how to read their charts.

Learning Charts

In this chapter, we introduce you
to 14 stitches that are the building
blocks of Tunisian Crochet stitch
patterns. Spend a little time getting
familiar with each stitch, and then you'll
be ready to progress into more complex
patterns in the chapters that follow.
You'll find the master symbol list and
guide to reading charts indispensable.

Experiment

Try the stitch pattern you chose with different yarns and different hooks for the right look you want for your project.

Create

Create your own one-of-a-kind project.

Each chapter introduces you to symbols used in charted Tunisian crochet. Once you have learned the basic stitches, you can increase your knowledge in the Typical, Color, and Lace Stitches.

As an aid to learning, the Scarf on page 84, has complete written instructions plus a chart showing each stitch pattern used. This project is a perfect example of experimenting with different yarns and hooks. Although the stitch pattern used is from the Color chapter, the project is worked in only one color with a larger hook, giving it a more lacy look.

Each row of Tunisian crochet is worked in two parts; a forward pass and a return pass. Whether you are right- or left-handed, the forward pass will always be read from right to left and the return pass will be read from left to right. As you will not be turning your work, the chart is always read as it is printed.

The final row of Tunisian crochet project is a binding off row. This is not shown on the charts. The type of binding off you desire, or even whether you choose not to include a binding off row, is a personal choice. For the most part, most stitch patterns can be bound off in slip stitch, inserting your hook as for Tunisian Simple Stitch (tss) or in the same predominant stitch of your stitch pattern. You can also bind off in single crochet, double crochet or in any stitch of your choosing.

Multiples

Multiples are the number of stitches required to work a pattern.

How to Read A Chart

- Each chart will show the beginning chains in the lower row of boxes (1). Chain the number of stitches indicated by the multiple given below the title for each stitch. For the chart below, you can chain any amount to begin.

- A Tunisian row is charted as a pair of boxes with the row number or F for the Foundation Row in the right hand column (2).

- The lower set of boxes for a row is the Forward Pass (3).

- The upper set of boxes for a row is the Return Pass (4).

- The stitch repeat, if applicable, is indicated on the bottom edge of the charts; for example Stitch 7, page 18.

- The Key contains all the stitches used and the hook insertions needed for a stitch if applicable. A complete Master List of the symbols used are on pages 10 and 11.

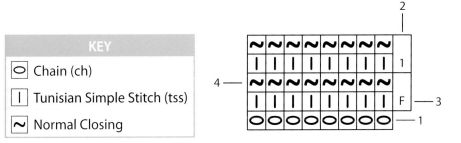

KEY	
O	Chain (ch)
I	Tunisian Simple Stitch (tss)
~	Normal Closing

Master List

Typical Hook Insertions

$\boxed{\mathsf{I}}$	Tunisian Simple Stitch (tss)
$\boxed{\downarrow}$	Tunisian Reverse Stitch (trs)
$\boxed{0}$	Tunisian Knit Stitch (tks)
$\boxed{\underline{0}}$	Tunisian Knit Stitch Purled
$\boxed{-}$	Tunisian Purl Stitch (tps)
$\boxed{\Phi}$	Tunisian Full Stitch (tfs)
$\boxed{\circ}$	Top of Closing Cluster
$\boxed{\phi}$	Top Horizontal Bar
◿ or ◺	2 stitches worked together
◿	2 Tunisian Double Stitches worked together
◺	2 stitches worked together Purled
△	3 stitches worked together
△	3 stitches worked together as for tss, then ch 1

Closing (Return Pass)

$\boxed{\sim}$	Normal Closing
~	Close 3 stitches together
○~○	Chain 1, close 3 stitches together, chain 1

- ▢ Chain (ch)
- ▢ Yarn Over (YO)
- ▢ Tunisian Extended Stitch (tes)
- ▢ Tunisian Double Stitch (tds)
- ▢ Tunisian Bobble Stitch (tbs)
- ▢ Tunisian 3-Double Stitch Bobble Stitch, with ch for a tes
- ▢ Tunisian Puff Stitch
- ▢ Tunisian Crossed Stitch, worked across 2 stitches
- ▢ Tunisian Double Crossed Stitch (2 tds crossed across 3 sts)
- ▢ Tunisian Twisted Stitch worked as for tss or tks
- ▢ Tunisian Twisted Stitch Purled
- ▢ Tunisian Extended Stitch (tes) worked as for tfs
- ▢ Tunisian Double Stitch (tds) worked as for tfs
- ▢ Pull loop through as indicated, yarn over, pull loop through as indicated (3 loops on hook)
- ▢ 2 Tunisian Double Stitches worked in same position (the number of tds indicates the number of stitches to work in the same position)
- ▢ Tunisian Slipped Stitch
- ▢ When left blank, there is a skipped stitch

Keys with the charts will indicate which hook insertion to use to create the stitches.

Can be worked on any number of chs.

	KEY
◯	Chain (ch)
I	Tunisian Simple Stitch (tss)
∼	Normal Closing

TUNISIAN SIMPLE STITCH
 (abbreviated tss)

Insert hook from **right** to **left** under next vertical bar *(Fig. 2, page 92)*, YO and pull up a loop.

Foundation Row: Pull up a loop in horizontal bar of second ch from hook and in each ch across, close *(Figs. 1a-c, page 91)*.

Row 1: Skip first vertical bar, work tss across, close.

Repeat Row 1 for pattern.

Can be worked on any number of chs.

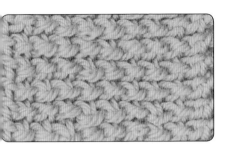

KEY

○	Chain (ch)
│	Tunisian Simple Stitch (tss)
↓	Tunisian Reverse Stitch (trs)
~	Normal Closing

—— STITCH GUIDE ——

TUNISIAN REVERSE STITCH
(abbreviated trs)

With hook at **back** of work, insert hook from **right** to **left** under next back vertical bar *(Fig. 5, page 92)*, YO and pull up a loop.

Foundation Row: Pull up a loop in horizontal bar of second ch from hook and in each ch across, close *(Figs. 1a-c, page 91)*.

Row 1: Skip first vertical bar, work trs across, close.

Repeat Row 1 for pattern.

Can be worked on any number of chs.

~	~	~	~	~	~	~	~	
Ọ	Ọ	Ọ	Ọ	Ọ	Ọ	Ọ	I	1
~	~	~	~	~	~	~	~	
I	I	I	I	I	I	I	I	F
⊙	⊙	⊙	⊙	⊙	⊙	⊙	⊙	

KEY	
⊙	Chain (ch)
I	Tunisian Simple Stitch (tss)
Ọ	Tunisian Knit Stitch (tks)
~	Normal Closing

—— STITCH GUIDE ——

TUNISIAN KNIT STITCH
  (abbreviated tks)

Insert hook from **front** to **back** between front and back vertical bars of next st *(Fig. 3, page 92)*, YO and pull up a loop.

Foundation Row: Pull up a loop in horizontal bar of second ch from hook and in each ch across, close. *(Figs. 1a-c, page 91)*.

Row 1: Skip first vertical bar, work tks across, close.

Repeat Row 1 for pattern.

Can be worked on any number of chs.

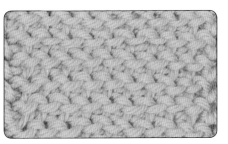

~	~	~	~	~	~	~	~	
—	—	—	—	—	—	—	│	1
~	~	~	~	~	~	~	~	
│	│	│	│	│	│	│	│	F
○	○	○	○	○	○	○	○	

KEY	
○	Chain (ch)
│	Tunisian Simple Stitch (tss)
—	Tunisian Purl Stitch (tps)
~	Normal Closing

STITCH GUIDE

TUNISIAN PURL STITCH
(abbreviated tps)

With yarn in **front** of work, insert hook from **right** to **left** under next vertical bar *(Fig. 6, page 93)*, YO and pull up a loop.

Foundation Row: Pull up a loop in horizontal bar of second ch from hook and in each ch across, close *(Figs. 1a-c, page 91)*.

Row 1: Skip the first vertical bar, work tps across, close.

Repeat Row 1 for pattern.

Can be worked on any number of chs.

~	~	~	~	~	~	~	~		
ℚ	ℚ	ℚ	ℚ	ℚ	ℚ	ℚ	ℚ	│	1
~	~	~	~	~	~	~	~		
│	│	│	│	│	│	│	│	│	F
⬭	⬭	⬭	⬭	⬭	⬭	⬭	⬭		

KEY	
⬭	Chain (ch)
│	Tunisian Simple Stitch (tss)
ℚ	Tunisian Twisted Stitch worked as for tks
~	Normal Closing

STITCH GUIDE

TUNISIAN TWISTED KNIT STITCH

Using the hook tip, pull the front next vertical bar over until you see the back vertical bar *(Fig. 7, page 93)*. Insert hook between vertical bars as for Tunisian Knit Stitch, YO and pull up a loop.

Foundation Row: Pull up a loop in horizontal bar of second ch from hook and in each ch across, close *(Figs. 1a-c, page 91)*.

Row 1: Skip the first vertical bar, work Tunisian Twisted Knit Stitch across, close.

Repeat Row 1 for pattern.

Can be worked on any number of chs.

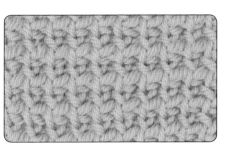

~	~	~	~	~	~	~	~		
Ω	Ω	Ω	Ω	Ω	Ω	Ω	|		1
~	~	~	~	~	~	~	~		
|	|	|	|	|	|	|	|		F
O	O	O	O	O	O	O	O		

KEY	
O	Chain (ch)
|	Tunisian Simple Stitch (tss)
Ω	Tunisian Twisted Stitch worked as for tss
~	Normal Closing

STITCH GUIDE

TUNISIAN TWISTED SIMPLE STITCH

Using the hook tip, grasp the next front vertical bar of next st, twist the hook down and around, forming a twist *(Fig. 8, page 93)*, YO and pull up a loop.

Foundation Row: Pull up a loop in horizontal bar of second ch from hook and in each ch across, close *(Figs. 1a-c, page 91)*.

Row 1: Skip the first vertical bar, work Tunisian Twisted Simple Stitch across, close.

Repeat Row 1 for pattern.

Chain a multiple of 2 chs.

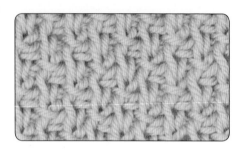

~	~	~	~	~	~	~	~	
Q	Q	Q	Q	Q	Q	Q	I	2
~	~	~	~	~	~	~	~	
Q	Q	Q	Q	Q	Q	Q	I	1
~	~	~	~	~	~	~	~	
I	I	I	I	I	I	I	I	F
O	O	O	O	O	O	O	O	

Repeat

KEY

O	Chain (ch)
I	Tunisian Simple Stitch (tss)
Q	Tunisian Knit Stitch (tks)
Q	Tunisian Knit Stitch Purled
~	Normal Closing

——— STITCH GUIDE ———

TUNISIAN KNIT STITCH
(abbreviated tks)

Insert hook from **front** to **back** between front and back vertical bars of next st *(Fig. 3, page 92)*, YO and pull up a loop.

TUNISIAN KNIT STITCH PURLED
(abbreviated tks purled)

With yarn in **front** of work, insert hook from **front** to **back** between front and back vertical bars *(Fig. 4, page 92)*, YO and pull up a loop.

Foundation Row: Pull up a loop in horizontal bar of second ch from hook and in each ch across, close *(Figs. 1a-c, page 91)*.

Row 1: Skip first vertical bar, work tks, (work tks purled, work tks) across, close.

Row 2: Skip first vertical bar, work tks purled, (work tks, work tks purled) across, close.

Repeat Rows 1 and 2 for pattern.

Chain a multiple of 3 + 2 chs.

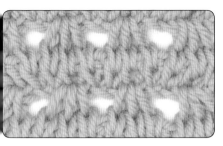

(Fig. 9, page 93)

Repeat

KEY

○	Chain (ch)
I	Tunisian Simple Stitch (tss)
ọ	Tunisian Extended Stitch (tes) worked as for tks
⊕	Top Horizontal Bar
⊖	Top of Closing Cluster
○~○	worked across 3 sts as follows: ch 1, close 3 sts together, ch 1
~	Normal Closing

STITCH GUIDE

TUNISIAN EXTENDED STITCH (abbreviated tes)

Insert hook from **front** to **back** between front and back vertical bars of next st, [YO *(Fig. 9, page 93)* and pull up a loop, YO and draw through one loop on hook (ch 1 made)].

Foundation Row: Pull up a loop in horizontal bar of second ch from hook and in each ch across, close *(Figs. 1a-c, page 91)*.

Row 1:
Step A (Forward Pass): Skip first vertical bar, ch 1 (**counts as first tes**), work tes across.
Step B (Return Pass): ★ Ch 2, YO and draw through 4 loops on hook (**Cluster made**); repeat from ★ across to last 2 loops on hook, ch 1, YO and draw through last 2 loops on hook.

Row 2: Skip first vertical bar, pull up a loop in next horizontal bar of ch and in each horizontal bar across *(Fig. 14, page 95)*, close.

Repeat Rows 1 and 2 for pattern.

Can be worked on any number of chs.

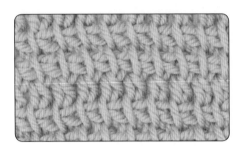

~	~	~	~	~	~	~	~	
I	I	I	I	I	I	I	I	2
~	~	~	~	~	~	~	~	
†	†	†	†	†	†	†	Ọ	1
~	~	~	~	~	~	~	~	
I	I	I	I	I	I	I	I	F
⊖	⊖	⊖	⊖	⊖	⊖	⊖	⊖	

KEY	
⊖	Chain (ch)
I	Tunisian Simple Stitch (tss)
Ọ	Tunisian Extended Stitch (tes)
†	Tunisian Double Stitch (tds) worked as for tss
~	Normal Closing

── STITCH GUIDE ──

TUNISIAN DOUBLE STITCH
   (abbreviated tds)

YO, insert hook from **right** to **left** under next vertical bar, YO and pull up a loop, YO and draw through 2 loops on hook *(Figs. 10a & b, page 94)*.

Foundation Row: Pull up a loop in horizontal bar of second ch from hook and in each ch across, close *(Figs. 1a-c, page 91)*.

Row 1: Ch 1 (**counts as first tes**), skip first vertical bar, work tds across, close.

Row 2: Skip first vertical bar, work tss across, close.

Repeat Rows 1 and 2 for pattern.

STITCH 10

Chain a multiple of 4 + 5 chs.

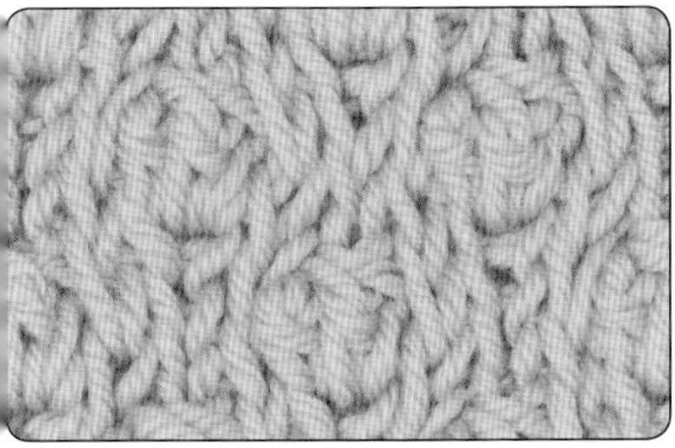

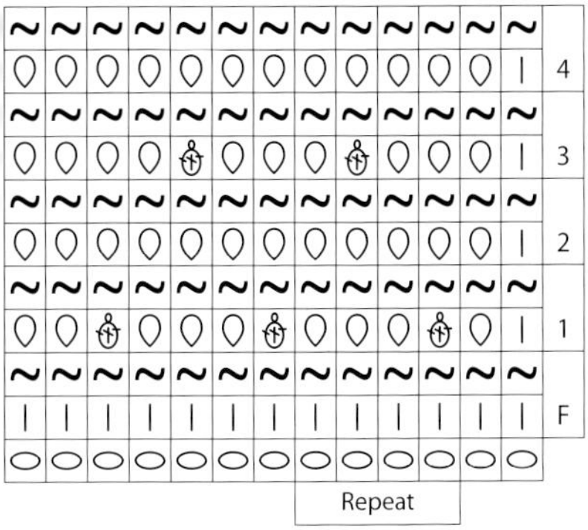

KEY

- Chain (ch)
- Tunisian Simple Stitch (tss)
- Tunisian Knit Stitch (tks)
- Tunisian Bobble Stitch (tbs) worked as for tks and tes
- Normal Closing

Foundation Row: Pull up a loop in horizontal bar of second ch from hook and in each ch across, close *(Figs. 1a-c, page 91)*.

Row 1: Skip first vertical bar, work tks, work tbs in next st, ★ work 3 tks, work tbs in next st; repeat from ★ across to last 2 sts, work 2 tks, close.

Row 2: Skip first vertical bar, work tks across, close.

Row 3: Skip first vertical bar, (work 3 tks, work tbs in next st) across to last 4 sts, work 4 tks, close.

Row 4: Skip first vertical bar, work tks across, close.

Repeat Rows 1-4 for pattern.

STITCH GUIDE

TUNISIAN DOUBLE STITCH

(abbreviated tds)

YO, insert hook from **front** to **back**, between front and back vertical bars of next st, YO and pull up a loop, YO and draw through 2 loops on hook *(Figs. 10a & b, page 94)*.

TUNISIAN BOBBLE STITCH

(abbreviated tbs)

Work 3 tds in st indicated, YO and draw through 3 loops on hook *(Figs. 11a & b, page 94)*.

Chain a multiple of 2 + 3 chs.

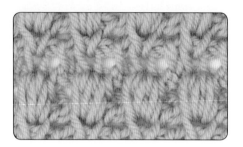

—— STITCH GUIDE ——

TUNISIAN KNIT STITCH
(abbreviated tks)

Insert hook from **front** to **back**, between front and back vertical bars of next st *(Fig. 3, page 92)*, YO and pull up a loop.

Foundation Row: Pull up a loop in horizontal bar of second ch from hook and in each ch across, close *(Figs. 1a-c, page 91)*.

Row 1: Skip first vertical bar, ★ YO, skip next stitch, work tks; repeat from ★ across, close.

Row 2:

Step A (Forward Pass): Skip first 2 vertical bars, (YO, work tks) 3 times in next st **(Puff St begun)**, ★ skip next st, (YO, work tks) 3 times in next st **(Puff St begun)**; repeat from ★ across to last 2 sts, skip next st, work tks.

Step B (Return Pass): Ch 2, ★ YO and draw through 7 loops on hook **(Puff St closed)**, ch 1; repeat from ★ across to last 2 loops on hook, YO and draw through last 2 loops on hook.

Row 3: Skip first vertical bar, ★ pull up a loop in horizontal bar of next st and in each st across to last st, work tss, close.

Repeat Rows 1-3 for pattern.

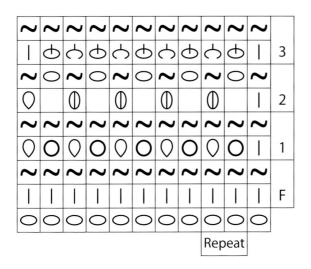

KEY

⬯ Chain (ch)		⏁ Top of Closing Cluster	
∣ Tunisian Simple Stitch (tss)		☐ Skipped stitch (intentionally left blank)	
O Yarn over (as used for a stitch) (YO)		◍ = ⬯ + ◊ + ⬯ + ◊ + ⬯ + ◊ Tunisian Puff Stitch worked as for tks; worked in same stitch, creates 6 loops on hook	
◊ Tunisian Knit Stitch (tks)		∼ Normal Closing	
⏁ Top Horizontal Bar			

Chain a multiple of 4 + 5 chs.

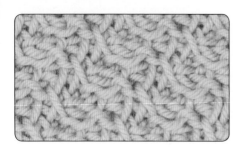

—— STITCH GUIDE ——

TUNISIAN PURL STITCH
  (abbreviated tps)
With yarn in **front** of work, insert hook from **right** to **left** under next vertical bar *(Fig. 6, page 93)*, YO and pull up a loop.

TUNISIAN CROSSED STITCH
  (uses 2 sts)
Skip next vertical bar, insert hook from **right** to **left** under next vertical bar, YO and pull up a loop, insert hook from **right** to **left** under skipped vertical bar, YO and pull up a loop *(Figs. 12a & b, page 94)*.

Foundation Row: Pull up a loop in horizontal bar of second ch from hook and in each ch across, close *(Figs. 1a-c, page 91)*.

Row 1: Skip first vertical bar, (work 2 tps, work Tunisian Crossed St) across to last 4 sts, work 4 tps, close.

Row 2: Skip first vertical bar, work tps, work Tunisian Crossed St, (work 2 tps, work Tunisian Crossed St) across to last st, work tps, close.

Row 3: Skip first vertical bar, (work Tunisian Crossed St, work 2 tps) across, close.

Row 4: Skip first vertical bar, work 3 tps, work Tunisian Crossed St, (work 2 tps, work Tunisian Crossed St) across to last 3 sts, work 3 tps, close.

Repeat Rows 1-4 for pattern.

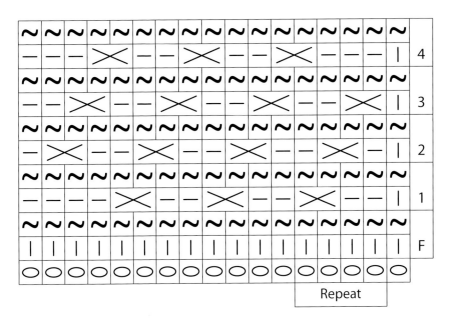

	Repeat	

Chain a multiple of 3 + 2 chs.

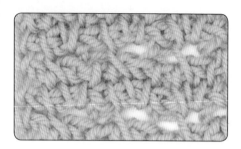

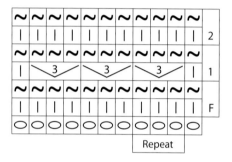

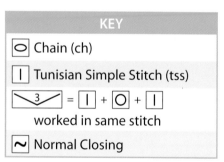

Repeat

KEY	
O	Chain (ch)
I	Tunisian Simple Stitch (tss)
$\diagdown 3 \diagup$ = I + O + I worked in same stitch	
~	Normal Closing

Foundation Row: Pull up a loop in horizontal bar of second ch from hook and in each ch across, close *(Figs. 1a-c, page 91)*.

Row 1: Skip first 2 vertical bars, insert hook under next vertical bar, YO and pull up a loop, YO, insert hook under same vertical bar, YO and pull up a loop (3 sts made from one), ★ skip next 2 vertical bars, insert hook under **next** vertical bar, YO and pull up a loop, YO, insert hook under same vertical bar, YO and pull up a loop (3 sts made from one); repeat from ★ across to last 2 sts, skip next vertical bar, work tss; close.

Row 2: Skip first vertical bar, work tss across, close.

Repeat Rows 1 and 2 for pattern.

Chain a multiple of 2 chs.

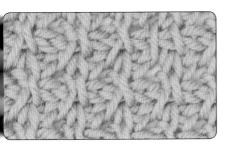

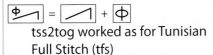

KEY

⬭	Chain (ch)
│	Tunisian Simple Stitch (tss)
—	Tunisian Purl Stitch (tps)

$\boxed{\Phi\diagdown}$ = $\boxed{\diagup}$ + $\boxed{\Phi}$
tss2tog worked as for Tunisian Full Stitch (tfs)

∼	Normal Closing

TUNISIAN FULL STITCH
(abbreviated tfs)
Insert hook from **front** to **back** under horizontal bar **between** two sts *(Fig. 14, page 95)*, YO and pull up a loop.

TUNISIAN SIMPLE STITCH 2 TOGETHER *(abbreviated tss2tog)*
Insert hook from **right** to **left** under next 2 vertical bars, YO and pull up a loop *(Figs. 17a & b, page 96)*.

TUNISIAN PURL STITCH
(abbreviated tps)
With yarn in **front** of work, insert hook from **right** to **left** under next vertical bar *(Fig. 6, page 93)*, YO and pull up a loop.

Foundation Row: Pull up a loop in horizontal bar of second ch from hook and in each ch across, close *(Figs. 1a-c, page 91)*.

Row 1: Skip first vertical bar, (work tss2tog, work tfs) across to last st, work tss, close.

Row 2: Skip first vertical bar, work tps, (work tss, work tps) across, close.

Repeat Rows 1 and 2 for pattern.

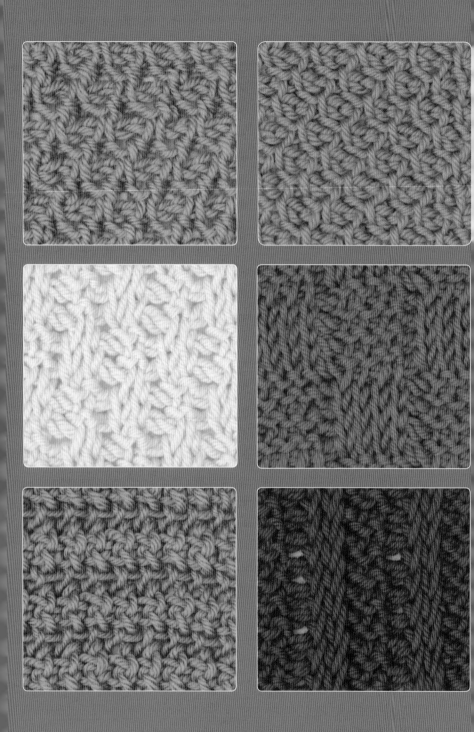

Chapter 2

Here you go beyond the basic stitches, with 17 richly textured pattern stitches presented in the typical format for charted Tunisian Crochet.

Typical Stitches

When you are ready for more variety, this assortment of pattern stitches uses twists, purls, double stitches, and other tricks to challenge you. Choose an easy pattern that repeats just a few rows, or branch out with a more-involved one that offers a hint of hearts or a checkerboard look. You'll return to this collection time after time to add excitement to scarves, afghans, and other items.

STITCH 15

Chain a multiple of 2 chs.

Repeat Rows 1 and 2 for pattern.

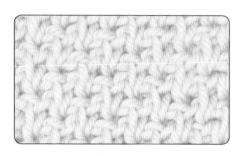

~	~	~	~	~	~	~	~	
⓪	⓪	⏊	⓪	⏊	⓪	⏊	I	2
~	~	~	~	~	~	~	~	
⓪	⏊	⓪	⏊	⓪	⏊	⓪	I	1
~	~	~	~	~	~	~	~	
I	I	I	I	I	I	I	I	F
ⓞ	ⓞ	ⓞ	ⓞ	ⓞ	ⓞ	ⓞ	ⓞ	

Repeat

KEY	
ⓞ	Chain (ch)
I	Tunisian Simple Stitch (tss)
⏊	Tunisian Reverse Stitch (trs)
⓪	Tunisian Knit Stitch (tks)
~	Normal Closing

STITCH 16

Chain a multiple of 2 chs.

Repeat Rows 1 and 2 for pattern.

~	~	~	~	~	~	~	~	
I	—	I	—	I	—	I	I	2
~	~	~	~	~	~	~	~	
—	I	—	I	—	I	—	I	1
~	~	~	~	~	~	~	~	
I	I	I	I	I	I	I	I	F
ⓞ	ⓞ	ⓞ	ⓞ	ⓞ	ⓞ	ⓞ	ⓞ	

Repeat

KEY	
ⓞ	Chain (ch)
I	Tunisian Simple Stitch (tss)
—	Tunisian Purl Stitch (tps)
~	Normal Closing

STITCH 17

Chain a multiple of 5 + 4 chs.

Repeat Row 1 for pattern.

KEY

O	Chain (ch)
I	Tunisian Simple Stitch (tss)
Q	Tunisian Knit Stitch (tks)
⌒≈⌒	worked across 3 sts as follows: ch 1, close 3 sts together, ch 1
⌒	Top Horizontal Bar
⌒	Top of Closing Cluster
~	Normal Closing

STITCH 18

Chain a multiple of 4 chs.

Repeat Row 1 for pattern.

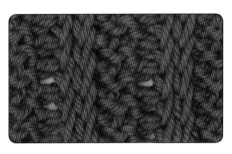

KEY

O	Chain (ch)
I	Tunisian Simple Stitch (tss)
—	Tunisian Purl Stitch (tps)
Q	Tunisian Twisted Stitch worked as for tks
~	Normal Closing

Chain a multiple of 4 chs.

Repeat Rows 1-4 for pattern.

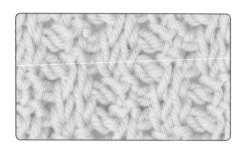

~	~	~	~	~	~	~	~	~	~	~	~	~	~	~	~	
Q	Q	Q	—	—	Q	Q	—	—	Q	Q	—	—	Q	Q	I	4
~	~	~	~	~	~	~	~	~	~	~	~	~	~	~	~	
Q	Q	Q	—	—	Q	Q	—	—	Q	Q	—	—	Q	Q	I	3
~	~	~	~	~	~	~	~	~	~	~	~	~	~	~	~	
Q	—	—	Q	Q	—	—	Q	Q	—	—	Q	Q	—	—	I	2
~	~	~	~	~	~	~	~	~	~	~	~	~	~	~	~	
Q	—	—	Q	Q	—	—	Q	Q	—	—	Q	Q	—	—	I	1
~	~	~	~	~	~	~	~	~	~	~	~	~	~	~	~	
I	I	I	I	I	I	I	I	I	I	I	I	I	I	I	I	F
O	O	O	O	O	O	O	O	O	O	O	O	O	O	O	O	

Repeat

KEY	
O	Chain (ch)
I	Tunisian Simple Stitch (tss)
Q	Tunisian Knit Stitch (tks)
—	Tunisian Purl Stitch (tps)
~	Normal Closing

Chain a multiple of 2 + 1 ch.

Repeat Rows 1 and 2 for pattern.

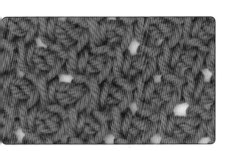

~	~	~	~	~	~	~	~	~	~	~	~	~	
I	Q	—	Q	—	Q	—	Q	—	Q	—	Q	I	2
~	~	~	~	~	~	~	~	~	~	~	~	~	
Q	—	Q	—	Q	—	Q	—	Q	—	Q	—	Q	1
~	~	~	~	~	~	~	~	~	~	~	~	~	
I	I	I	I	I	I	I	I	I	I	I	I	I	F
O	O	O	O	O	O	O	O	O	O	O	O	O	

Repeat

KEY	
O	Chain (ch)
I	Tunisian Simple Stitch (tss)
—	Tunisian Purl Stitch (tps)
Q	Tunisian Extended Stitch (tes) worked as for tks
~	Normal Closing

Chain a multiple of 2 chs.

Repeat Rows 1-4 for pattern.

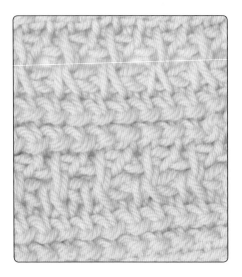

KEY	
O	Chain (ch)
I	Tunisian Simple Stitch (tss)
⊥	Tunisian Reverse Stitch (trs)
⅌	Top Horizontal Bar
∿° = O + ⟍	Yarn over, tss2tog
∿	Normal Closing

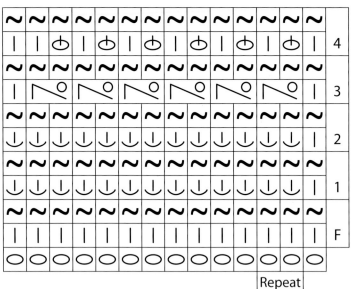

Chain a multiple of 6 + 5 chs.

Repeat Rows 1-4 for pattern.

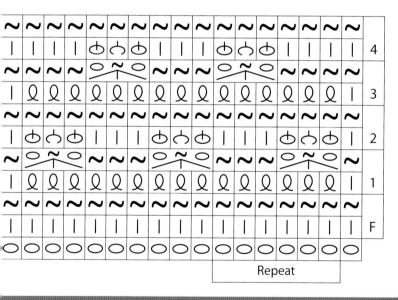

KEY

⭕ Chain (ch)	ℓ Tunisian Twisted Stitch worked as for tss
	⊶̃⊶ worked across 3 sts as follows: ch 1, close 3 sts together, ch 1
| Tunisian Simple Stitch (tss)	
⏧ Top Horizontal Bar	∿ Normal Closing
⏥ Top of Closing Cluster	

Chain a multiple of 3 + 2 chs.

Repeat Row 1 for pattern.

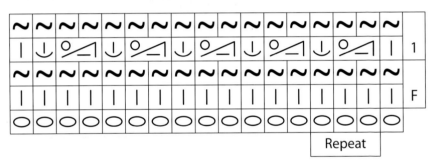

Repeat

KEY
Chain (ch)
Tunisian Simple Stitch (tss)
Tunisian Reverse Stitch (trs)
= + with yarn in front, tss2tog (wrapped), Yarn over (YO)
Normal Closing

Chain a multiple of 10 + 9 chs.

Repeat Rows 1-10 for pattern.

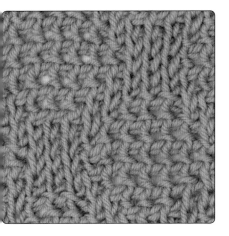

KEY	
◯	Chain (ch)
I	Tunisian Simple Stitch (tss)
Ọ	Tunisian Knit Stitch (tks)
Ọ	Tunisian Knit Stitch Purled
∼	Normal Closing

Repeat

STITCH 25	STITCH 26
Can be worked on any number of chs. Repeat Rows 1 and 2 for pattern.	Chain a multiple of 12 + 5 chs. Repeat Rows 3-16 for pattern.

~	~	~	~	~	~		
0̸	Φ	Φ	Φ	Φ		I	2
~	~	~	~	~ ~			
0̸	Φ	Φ	Φ	Φ	I		1
~ ~	~	~	~	~			
I I	I	I	I	I		F
O O	O	O	O	O		

KEY

O	Chain (ch)
I	Tunisian Simple Stitch (tss)
Φ	Tunisian Full Stitch (tfs)
0̸	Tunisian Knit Stitch (tks)
~	Normal Closing

KEY

O	Chain (ch)
I	Tunisian Simple Stitch (tss)
↓	Tunisian Reverse Stitch (trs)
0̸	Tunisian Knit Stitch (tks)
~	Normal Closing

Note: Since the tfs is worked between stitches, the chart is offset.

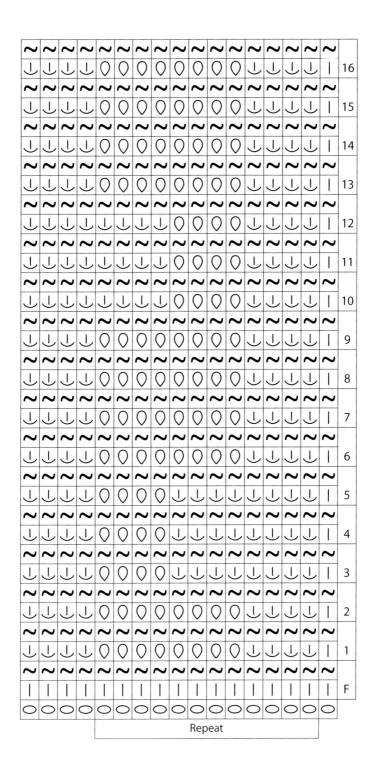

Chain a multiple of 19 + 4 chs.

Repeat Rows 1-17 for pattern.

KEY	
O	Chain (ch)
I	Tunisian Simple Stitch (tss)
↓	Tunisian Reverse Stitch (trs)
Q	Tunisian Knit Stitch (tks)
~	Normal Closing

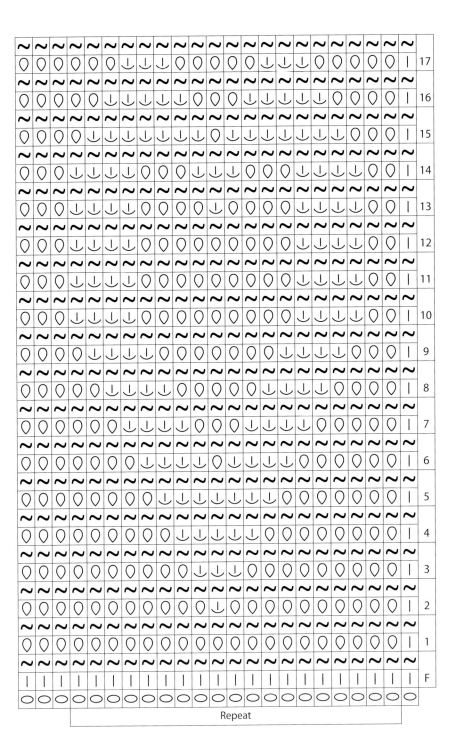

41

Chain a multiple of 2 chs.

Repeat Rows 1 and 2 for pattern.

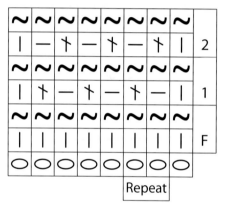

~	~	~	~	~	~	~	~	
I	—	†	—	†	—	†	I	2
~	~	~	~	~	~	~	~	
I	†	—	†	—	†	—	I	1
~	~	~	~	~	~	~	~	
I	I	I	I	I	I	I	I	F
O	O	O	O	O	O	O	O	

Repeat

KEY	
O	Chain (ch)
I	Tunisian Simple Stitch (tss)
†	Tunisian Double Stitch (tds) worked as for tss
—	Tunisian Purl Stitch (tps)
~	Normal Closing

Chain a multiple of 8 + 6 chs.

Repeat Rows 1-8 for pattern.

Row
8
7
6
5
4
3
2
1
F

Repeat

KEY	
⊙ Chain (ch)	✕ Tunisian Cross Stitch worked as for tss
	Tunisian Simple Stitch (tss)	∿ Normal Closing
— Tunisian Purl Stitch (tps)	

Chain a multiple of 2 chs.

Repeat Rows 1 and 2 for pattern.

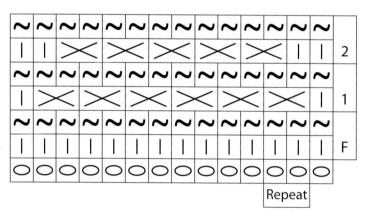

~	~	~	~	~	~	~	~	~	~	~	~	~	~	~
I	I	✕	✕	✕	✕	✕	I	I						2

Repeat

KEY

O	Chain (ch)
I	Tunisian Simple Stitch (tss)
✕	Tunisian Cross Stitch worked as for tss
~	Normal Closing

STITCH 31

Chain a multiple of 8 + 6 chs.

Repeat Rows 1-8 for pattern.

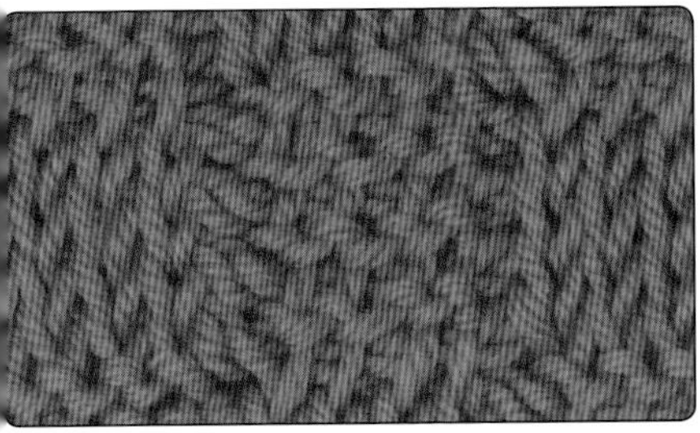

KEY	
○	Chain (ch)
|	Tunisian Simple Stitch (tss)
—	Tunisian Purl Stitch (tps)
0	Tunisian Knit Stitch (tks)
~	Normal Closing

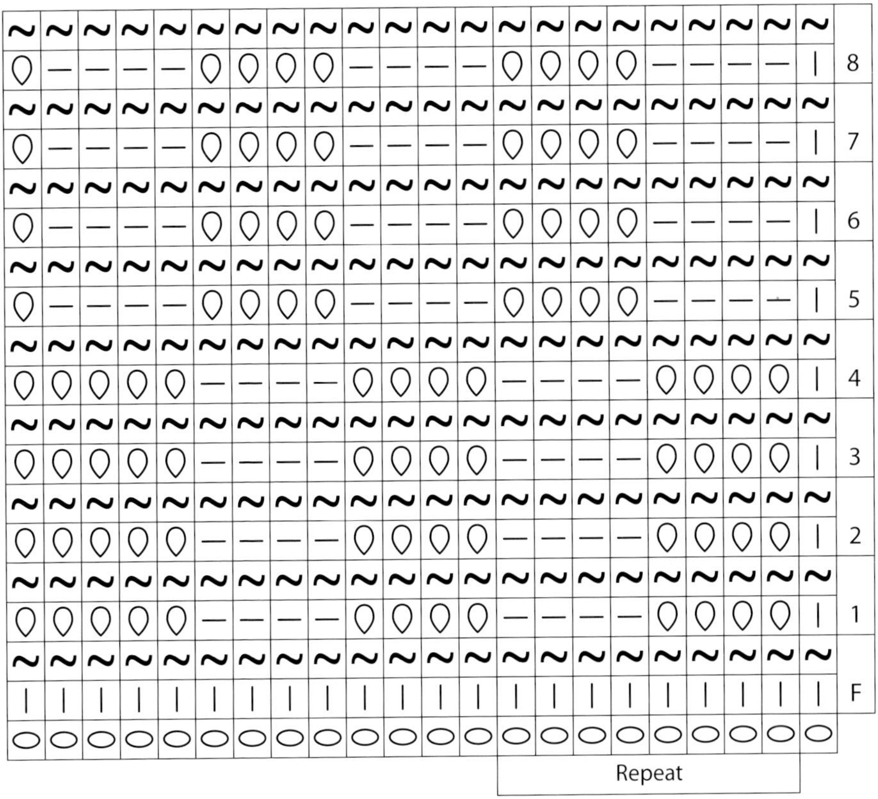

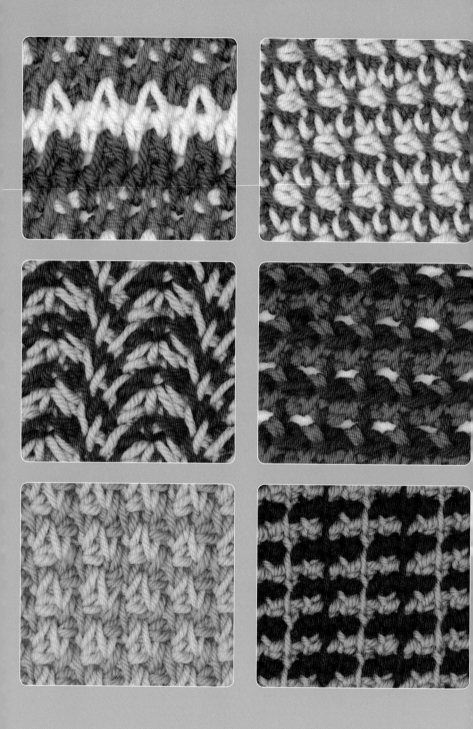

This chapter presents a collection of 12 pattern stitches that combine two or three yarn colors.

Color Stitches

You can always count on color to add pizzazz to your crochet! Each of these 12 pattern stitches proves what a dramatic change it can make when you combine color with different stitches. Those with a shorter height create a somewhat tweedy effect, while tall or extended stitches give more definition. But don't forget that you also can work these patterns in a single color, as we did by using Stitch 40 for the Scarf on page 84 – who would have guessed!

Chain a multiple of 6 + 11 chs.

Repeat Row 1 for pattern.

Note: Change colors at end of row (Forward Pass) *(Fig. 18b, page 96).*

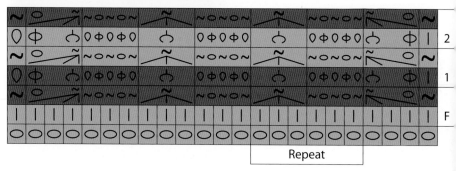

Repeat

KEY
⃝ Chain (ch)
I Tunisian Simple Stitch (tss)
Q Tunisian Knit Stitch (tks)
⏀ Tunisian Full Stitch (tfs)
⭒ Top of Closing Cluster
⁓ close 3 sts together
∾ Normal Closing

Chain a multiple of 2 chs.

Repeat Rows 1 and 2 for pattern.

Note: Change colors at end of row (Forward Pass) *(Fig. 18b, page 96)*.

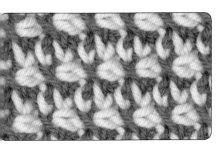

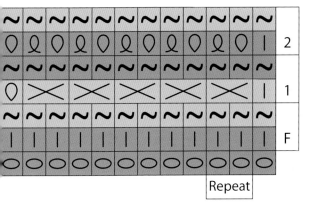

KEY	
◯	Chain (ch)
		Tunisian Simple Stitch (tss)
Ọ	Tunisian Knit Stitch (tks)
Ǫ	Tunisian Twisted Stitch worked as for tss
✕	Tunisian Crossed Stitch
∼	Normal Closing

Chain a multiple of 2 chs.

Repeat Rows 1 and 2 for pattern.

Note: Change colors at end of row (Forward Pass) *(Fig. 18b, page 96)*.

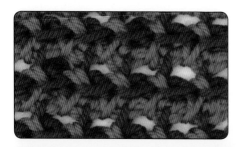

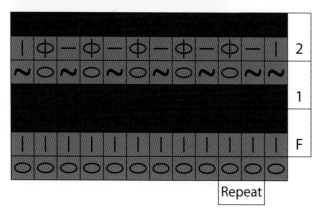

Repeat

KEY	
O	Chain (ch)
I	Tunisian Simple Stitch (tss)
Φ	Tunisian Full Stitch (tfs)
—	Tunisian Purl Stitch (tps)
◿	with yarn in front, tss2tog worked as for tss (wrapped)
∼	Normal Closing

Chain a multiple of 2 chs.

Repeat Rows 1 and 2 for pattern.

Note: Change colors at end of row (Forward Pass) *(Fig. 18b, page 96)*.

~	~	~	~	~	~	~	~	~	~	~	~	~	
I	Q	I	Q	I	Q	I	Q	I	Q	I	I		2
~	~	~	~	~	~	~	~	~	~	~	~	~	
I	I	Q	I	Q	I	Q	I	Q	I	Q	I		1
~	~	~	~	~	~	~	~	~	~	~	~	~	
I	I	I	I	I	I	I	I	I	I	I	I		F
O	O	O	O	O	O	O	O	O	O	O	O		

Repeat

	KEY
O	Chain (ch)
I	Tunisian Simple Stitch (tss)
Q	Tunisian Twisted Stitch worked as for tks
~	Normal Closing

Chain a multiple of 4 + 1 ch.

Repeat Rows 1 and 2 for pattern.

Note: Change colors at beginning of row (Return Pass) *(Fig. 18a, page 96)*.

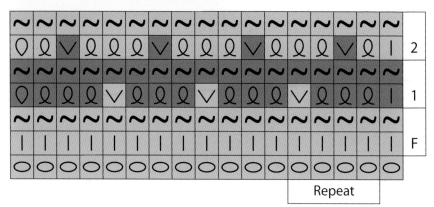

Repeat

KEY	
⬭	Chain (ch)
I	Tunisian Simple Stitch (tss)
Ⴓ	Tunisian Twisted Stitch worked as for tks
Ọ	Tunisian Knit Stitch (tks)
V	Tunisian Slip Stitch
∿	Normal Closing

Chain a multiple of 2 chs.

Repeat Rows 1 and 2 for pattern.

Note: Change colors at end of row (Forward Pass) *(Fig. 18b, page 96)*.

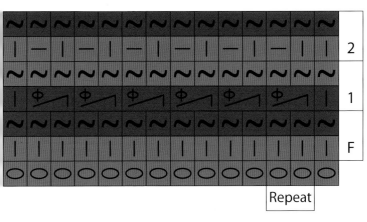

Repeat

KEY

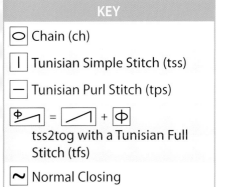

⬭	Chain (ch)
I	Tunisian Simple Stitch (tss)
—	Tunisian Purl Stitch (tps)

tss2tog with a Tunisian Full Stitch (tfs)

| ~ | Normal Closing |

Chain a multiple of 6 + 5 chs.

Repeat Rows 1-4 for pattern.

Note: Change colors at end of row (Forward Pass) *(Fig. 18b, page 96)*.

KEY	
⊙	Chain (ch)
│	Tunisian Simple Stitch (tss)
0	Tunisian Knit Stitch (tks)
⊥	Tunisian Reverse Stitch (trs)
⟑	Top of Horizontal Bar
⟏	Top of Closing Cluster
⟋⟋⟋	worked across 3 sts as follows: ch 1, close 3 sts together, ch 1
∼	Normal Closing

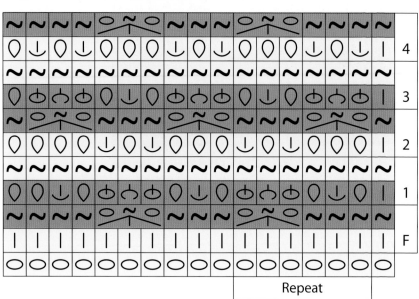

Repeat

Chain a multiple of 3 + 2 chs.

Repeat Rows 1-6 for pattern.

Note: Change colors at end of row (Forward Pass) *(Fig. 18b, page 96)*.

KEY

O	Chain (ch)
I	Tunisian Simple Stitch (tss)
↓	Tunisian Reverse Stitch (trs)
Q	Tunisian Extended Stitch (tes)
Q	Tunisian Knit Stitch Purled
Ω	Tunisian Twisted Stitch worked as for tss
†	Tunisian Double Stitch (tds) worked as for tss
✕	Tunisian Double Crossed Stitch skip next 2 sts, tds in next st, tds in first skipped st (center is unworked)
Φ	Tuinisian Full Stitch (tfs)
∼	Normal Closing

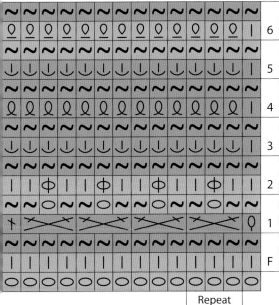

Chain a multiple of 3 + 2 chs.

Repeat Rows 1 and 2 for pattern.

Note: Change colors at beginning of row (Return Pass) *(Fig. 18a, page 96).*

KEY	
⬭	Chain (ch)
⎮	Tunisian Simple Stitch (tss)

 = ⟋⟍ + ⟍⟋ ₃

Insert hook as for tss in next 3 sts, YO and pull up a loop, YO, insert hook in same 3 sts, YO and pull up a loop (3 loops made)

| ∼ | Normal Closing |

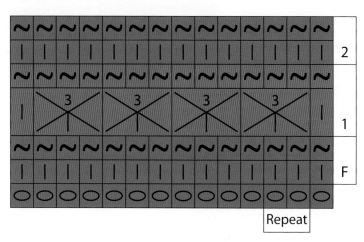

Chain a multiple of 2 chs.

Repeat Rows 1-4 for pattern.

Note: Change colors at end of row (Forward Pass) *(Fig. 18b, page 96).*

	KEY
O	Chain (ch)
I	Tunisian Simple Stitch (tss)
Q	Tunisian Twisted Stitch worked as for tss
✕	Tunisian Cross Stitch worked as for tss
V	Tunisian Slip Stitch
⧗ = ⧸ + ⧗	tss2tog worked as for tss, then work tfs as for tes (ch after loop has been pulled up)
~	Normal Closing

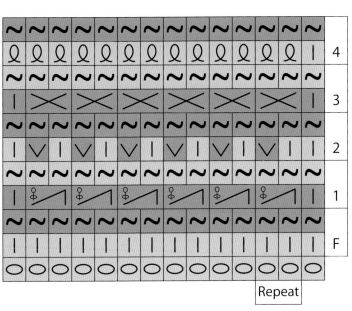

Repeat

Chain a multiple of 2 chs.

Repeat Row 1 for pattern.

Note: Change colors at beginning (Return Pass) *(Fig. 18a, page 96)* and end of row (Forward Pass) *(Fig. 18b, page 96)*.

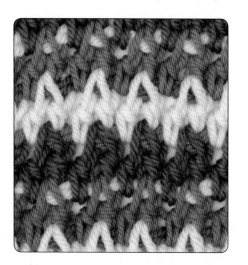

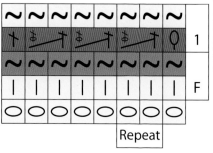

							KEY

⬭	Chain (ch)
│	Tunisian Simple Stitch (tss)
⭗	Tunisian Extended Stitch (tes)
φ	Tunisian Full Stitch (tfs)

tds2tog worked as for tss then tds worked as for tfs

| ~ | Normal Closing |

Chain a multiple of 2 chs.

Repeat Rows 1 and 2 for pattern.

Note: Change colors at beginning (Return Pass) *(Fig. 18a, page 96)* and end of row (Forward Pass) *(Fig. 18b, page 96)*.

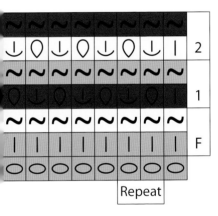

KEY	
⭕	Chain (ch)
│	Tunisian Simple Stitch (tss)
◯	Tunisian Knit Stitch (tks)
↓	Tunisian Reverse Stitch (trs)
～	Normal Closing

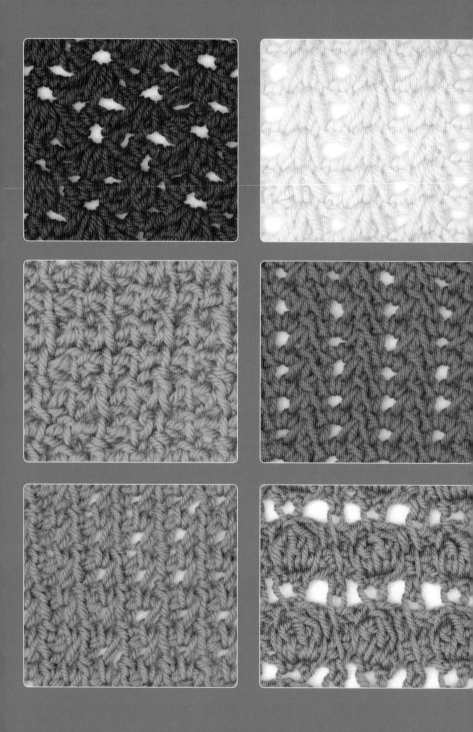

Whether dense or airy, these 18 lace patterns let you add romantic style to your Tunisian Crochet.

Lace Stitches

Tunisian Crochet is perhaps best known as a dense fabric that makes sturdy, practical afghans. Yet it can also have a lacy quality, as these 18 pattern stitches show. You'll find shell looks, crossed stitches, extended stitches, clustered stitches, and bobbles all contributing their special features to create the lace effects, including some that resemble trees and pineapples.

Chain a multiple of 3 chs.

Repeat Rows 1 and 2 for pattern.

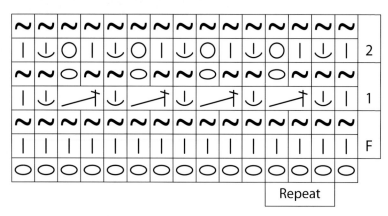

Repeat

KEY	
O	Chain (ch)
I	Tunisian Simple Stitch (tss)
⊥	Tunisian Reverse Stitch (trs)
⌐⊤	tds2tog worked as for tss
O	Yarn Over (as used for a st) (YO)
~	Normal Closing

Chain a multiple of 3 + 2 chs.

Repeat Row 1 for pattern.

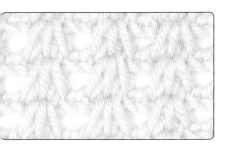

KEY	
O	Chain (ch)
I	Tunisian Simple Stitch (tss)
⟀	Top Horizontal Bar
⟁	Top of Closing Cluster
O~O	worked across 3 sts as follows: ch 1, close 3 sts together, ch 1
~	Normal Closing

Chain a multiple of 3 + 2 chs.

Repeat Rows 1 and 2 for pattern.

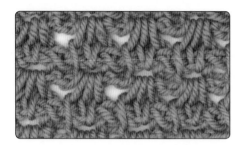

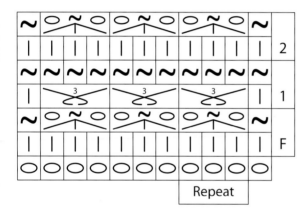

Repeat

KEY	
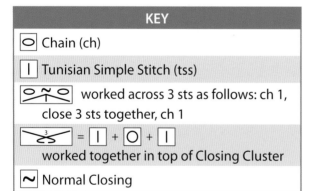 O	Chain (ch)
I	Tunisian Simple Stitch (tss)
⊙⁓⊙	worked across 3 sts as follows: ch 1, close 3 sts together, ch 1
✕₃ = I + O + I	worked together in top of Closing Cluster
⁓	Normal Closing

Chain a multiple of 3 + 2 chs.

Repeat Row 1 for pattern.

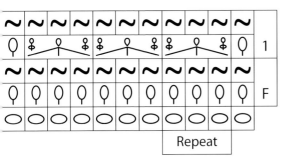

	KEY	
⌾	Chain (ch)	
♀	Tunisian Extended Stitch (tes)	
♂	Tunisian Extended Stitch (tes) worked as for tfs	

$$\text{♂ ⋀ ♂} = \text{♂} + \text{⋀} + \text{♂}$$

tes worked as for tfs, 3 sts worked together as for tss, then ch 1, tes worked as for tfs

~	Normal Closing

STITCH 48

Chain a multiple of 6 + 9 chs.

Repeat Rows 1 and 2 for pattern.

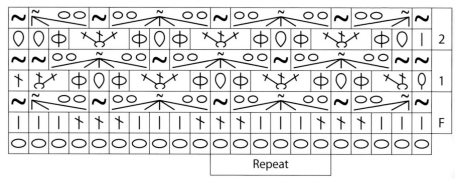

KEY		
Chain (ch)	Ch 2, close 5 sts together, ch 2	
Tunisian Simple Stitch (tss)	Close 3 sts together, ch 2	
Tunisian Knit Stitch (tks)	Ch 2, close 3 sts together	
Tunisian Full Stitch (tfs)	3 tds worked in Closing Cluster	
Tunisian Extended Stitch (tes)	2 tds worked in Closing Cluster	
Tunisian Double Stitch (tds) worked as for tks at end of row or into ch on foundation row	Normal Closing	

STITCH 49

Chain a multiple of 8 + 1 ch.

Repeat Rows 1 and 2 for pattern.

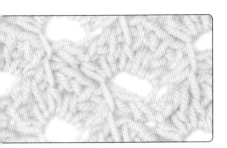

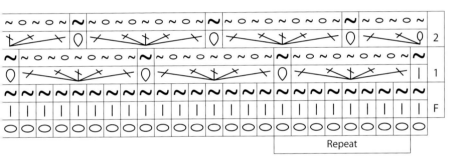

Repeat

KEY	
⬯ Chain (ch)	⤢⤡ Ch 1, work 2 tds in first st as for tks
▯ Tunisian Simple Stitch (tss)	⤢⤡ 5 tds worked as for tks in one st
⬯ Tunisian Knit Stitch (tks)	⤢ 3 tds worked as for tks in last st
⥮ Tunisian Double Stitch (tds) worked as for tks	∼ Normal Closing

STITCH 50

Chain a multiple of 6 + 2 chs.

Repeat Rows 1-12 for pattern.

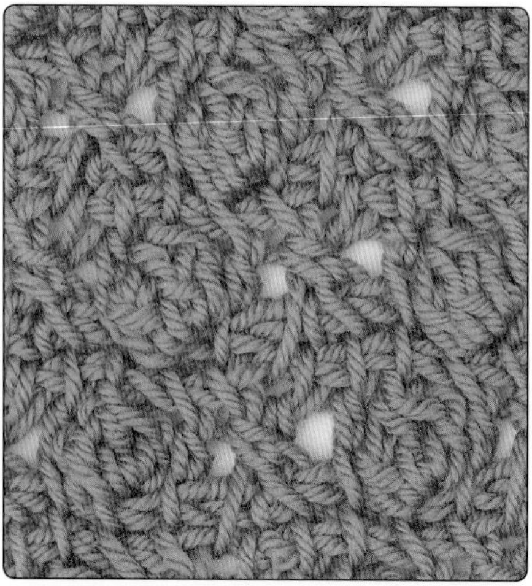

KEY
Chain (ch)
Tunisian Simple Stitch (tss)
Tunisian Extended Stitch (tes)
Tunisian Double Stitch (tds) worked as for tss
Tunisian Full Stitch (tfs)
Tunisian Bobble Stitch
Tunisian Double Crossed Stitch skip next 2 sts, tds in next st, tds in first skipped st (center is unworked)
Normal Closing

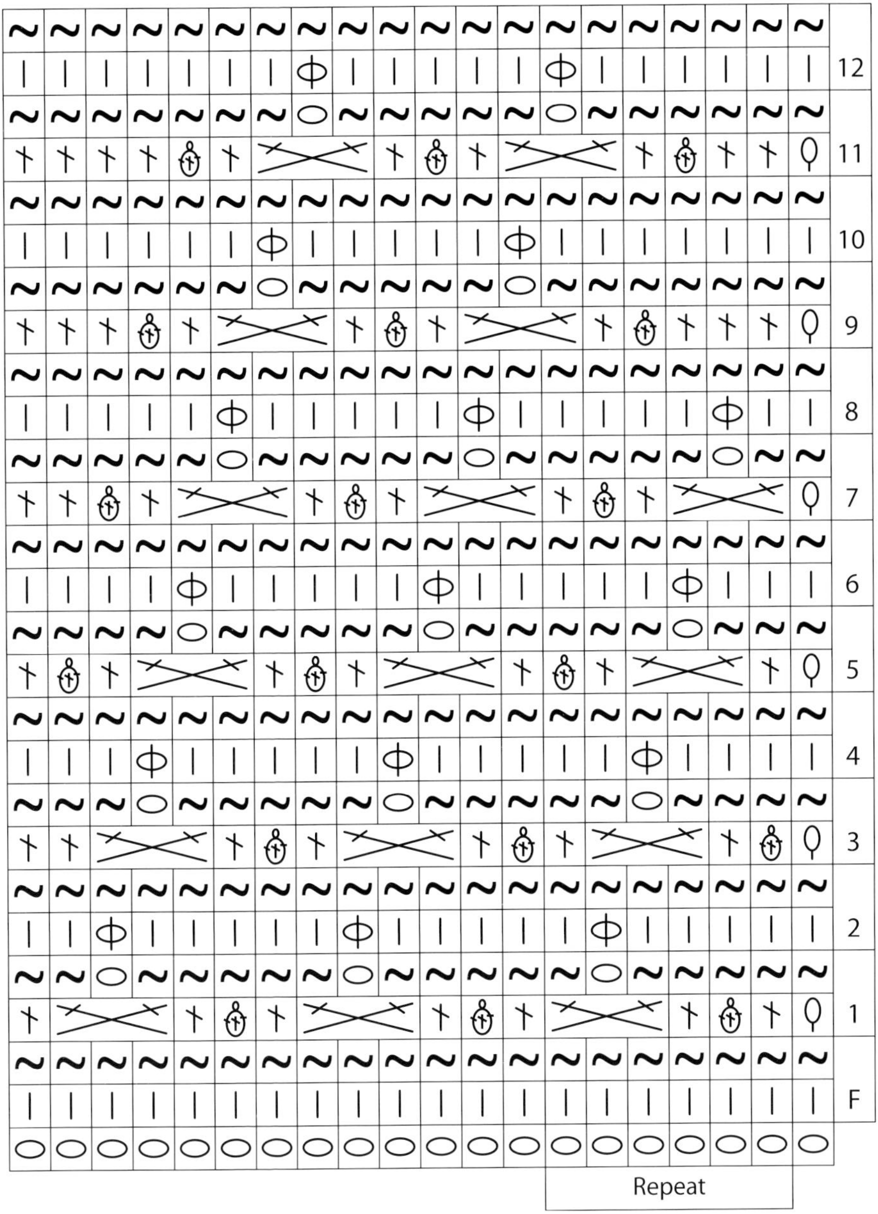

Knitting chart

Row
12
11
10
9
8
7
6
5
4
3
2
1
F

Repeat

Chain a multiple of 2 chs.

Repeat Row 1 for pattern.

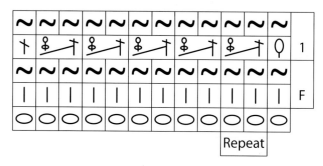

Repeat

KEY	
⬭	Chain (ch)
│	Tunisian Simple Stitch (tss)
ⵍ	Tunisian Extended Stitch (tes)
┼	Tunisian Double Stitch (tds)
ⵍ┼ = ╱┼ + ⵍ	
	tds2tog worked as for tss, then tes as for tfs
∼	Normal Closing

Chain a multiple of 2 chs.

Repeat Rows 1 and 2 for pattern.

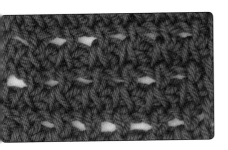

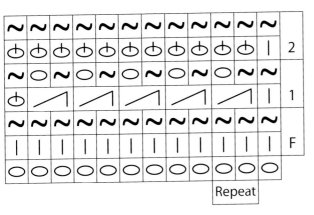

Repeat

KEY	
O	Chain (ch)
I	Tunisian Simple Stitch (tss)
⌽	Top Horizontal Bar
⟋	tss2tog worked as for tss
~	Normal Closing

Chain a multiple of 4 + 1 chs.

Repeat Rows 1 and 2 for pattern.

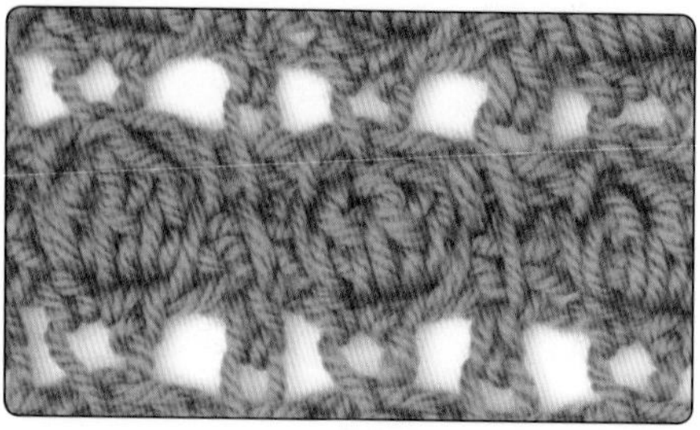

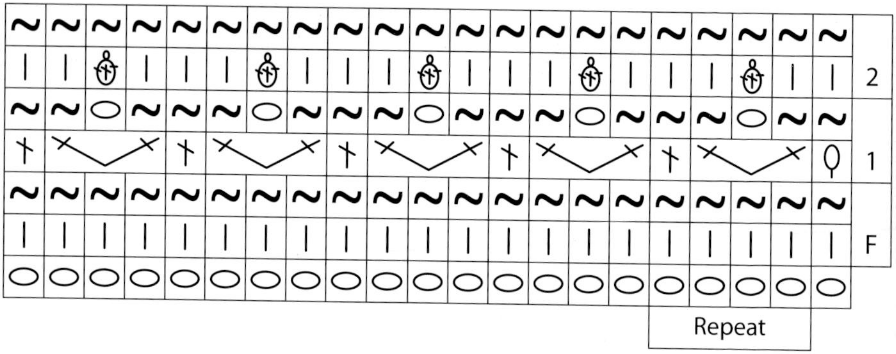

KEY
Chain (ch)
Tunisian Simple Stitch (tss)
Tunisian Extended Stitch (tes)
Tunisian Double Stitch (tds) worked as for tss
Tunisian Bobble Stitch (tbs) worked as for tfs and tes
skip next st, 2 tds worked as for tss in next st, skip next st
Tunisian Knit Stitch (tks)
Normal Closing

Chain a multiple of 3 + 2 chs.

Repeat Rows 1-3 for pattern.

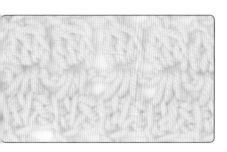

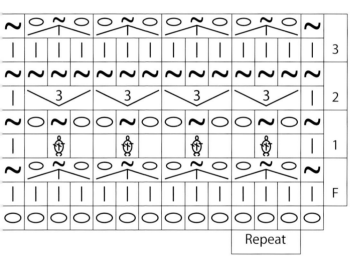

Repeat

KEY		
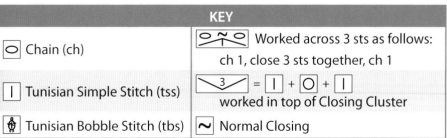		

Chain a multiple of 3 + 2 chs.

Repeat Row 2 for pattern.

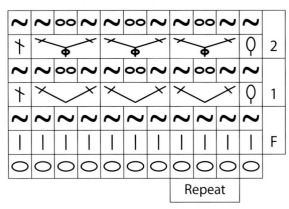

Repeat

KEY	
⬭ Chain (ch)	⤬〜⤬ skip next st, 2 tds worked as for tss in next st, skip next st
❙ Tunisian Simple Stitch (tss)	⤬💠⤬ skip next st, 2 tds worked as for tfs in same sp, skip next st
ⓞ Tunisian Extended Stitch (tes)	∞ Chain 2
✝ Tunisian Double Stitch (tds) worked as for tss	〜 Normal Closing

Chain a multiple of 3 + 2 chs.

Repeat Rows 1 and 2 for pattern.

KEY

⬭ Chain (ch)
	Tunisian Simple Stitch (tss)
⑨ Tunisian Extended Stitch (tes)
✝ Tunisian Double Stitch (tds) worked as for tss
✕✕ Tunisian Double Crossed Stitch skip next 2 sts, tds in next st, tds in first skipped st (center is unworked)
⏀ Tunisian Full Stitch (tfs)
∼ Normal Closing

Chain a multiple of 2 chs.

Repeat Rows 1 and 2 for pattern.

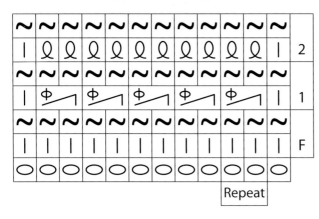

KEY	
⊙	Chain (ch)
I	Tunisian Simple Stitch (tss)
Ω	Tunisian Twisted Stitch worked as for tss
⟋⟍ = ⟋ + Φ	tss2tog worked as for tfs
∼	Normal Closing

Chain a multiple of 3 + 2 chs.

Repeat Rows 2 and 3 for pattern.

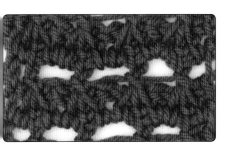

	KEY
⬭	Chain (ch)
		Tunisian Simple Stitch (tss)
⚯	Tunisian Extended Stitch (tes) worked as for tfs
⚲	Tunisian Extended Stitch (tes) worked as for tss
⟍⚲⟋	3 sts together as for tss, then ch 1
∾	Normal Closing

Chain a multiple of 10 + 5 chs.

Repeat Rows 6-11 for pattern.

KEY	
⃝ Chain (ch)	ᵛ̌³ = ▯ + ⃝ + ▯ worked as for tks
▮ Tunisian Simple Stitch (tss)	ᵞ̌³ = ▯ + ⃝ + ▯ worked as for tfs
▬ Tunisian Purl Stitch (tps)	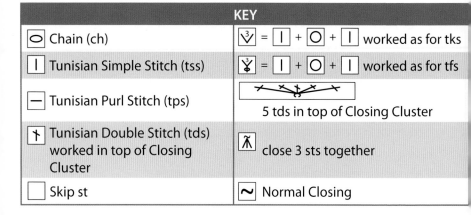 5 tds in top of Closing Cluster
✝ Tunisian Double Stitch (tds) worked in top of Closing Cluster	Ⱥ close 3 sts together
▯ Skip st	∼ Normal Closing

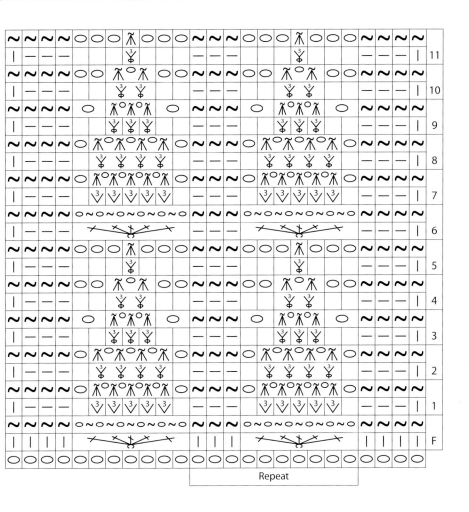

Chain a multiple of 12 + 5 chs.

Repeat Rows 4-7 for pattern.

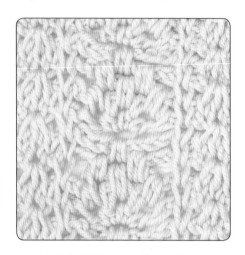

KEY		
⊖ Chain (ch)		� Top of Closing Cluster
▯ Tunisian Simple Stitch (tss)		⊝⊹⊝ worked across 3 sts as follows: ch 1, close 3 sts together, ch 1
▯ Tunisian Knit Stitch (tks)		⟱³ = ▯ + ⊖ + ▯ worked as for tfs
⟲ Top Horizontal Bar		☐ Skip st
† Tunisian Double Stitch (tds) worked in top of Closing Cluster		⋏ Close 3 sts together
⟋⟍⟱⟋⟍ 4 tds worked in top of Closing Cluster		∼ Normal Closing

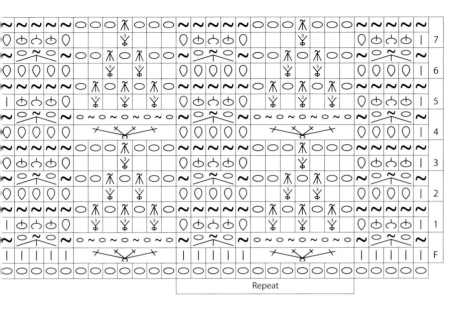

Repeat

Chain a multiple of 6 + 5 chs.

Repeat Rows 1-4 for pattern.

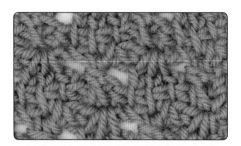

KEY	
☉ Chain (ch)	⟩⟨³ = □ + ☉ + □ worked together in top of Closing Cluster
□ Tunisian Simple Stitch (tss)	☉∿☉ worked across 3 sts as follows: ch 1, close 3 sts together, ch 1
☿ Tunisian Extended Stitch (tes) worked as for tss	⟩⟨ Tunisian Double Crossed Stitch skip next 2 sts, tds in next st, tds in first skipped st (center is unworked)
� Tunisian Full Stitch (tfs)	∿ Normal Closing
✝ Tunisian Double Stitch (tds) worked as for tss	

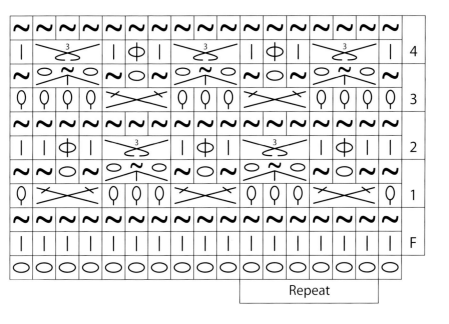

SCARF

Finished Size: 5½" wide x 59" long (14 cm x 150 cm)

SHOPPING LIST

Yarn (Light Weight)
[3.5 ounces, 307 yards
(100 grams, 281 meters) per
hank]:

☐ One hank

Tunisian Hook

Minimum length of 6" (15 cm)

☐ Size L (8 mm)
   or size needed for gauge

Model was made using Cascade
Venezia Sport.

GAUGE INFORMATION

In pattern, 20 sts = 5½" (10 cm);
8 rows = 4" (10 cm)

INSTRUCTIONS

Ch 20.

You can follow the chart on page 87
or the written instructions.

Foundation Row (Right side)**:** Insert
hook in horizontal bar of second ch
from hook, YO and pull up a loop,
★ insert hook in horizontal bar
of **next** ch, YO and pull up a loop;
repeat from ★ across, close.

Row 1: Skip first vertical bar,
★ insert hook from **right** to **left**
under each of next 3 vertical bars,
YO and pull up a loop, YO, insert
hook from **right** to **left** under same
3 vertical bars, YO and pull up a
loop; repeat from ★ across to last st,
tss in last st, close.

Row 2: Skip first vertical bar, work tss across, close.

Repeat Rows 1 and 2 until Scarf measures approximately 58¾" (149 cm) from beginning ch, ending by working Row 2.

Last Row: Ch 1, skip first vertical bar, working as for tss, sc in each st across; finish off.

Blocking helps to smooth your work and give it a professional appearance. Follow the yarn label's instructions for laundering before blocking. Pin out your piece to the correct size with rust-proof pins and allow to dry completely.

Repeat Rows 1-2 for pattern.

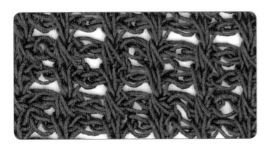

∼	∼	∼	∼	∼	∼	∼	∼	∼	∼	∼	∼	∼	∼	∼		
																2

(Chart showing Row 1 with 3-stitch crossed symbols, Row F, and foundation chain)

Repeat

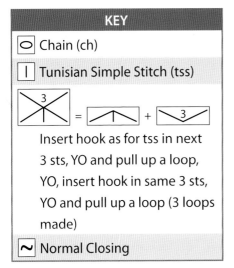

KEY

⬭ Chain (ch)

| Tunisian Simple Stitch (tss)

✕ = ∕ + ∖ — Insert hook as for tss in next 3 sts, YO and pull up a loop, YO, insert hook in same 3 sts, YO and pull up a loop (3 loops made)

∼ Normal Closing

TIP: For a different look, use two yarn colors as shown in Stitch 40 on page 56, the pattern stitch used for this single-color Scarf.

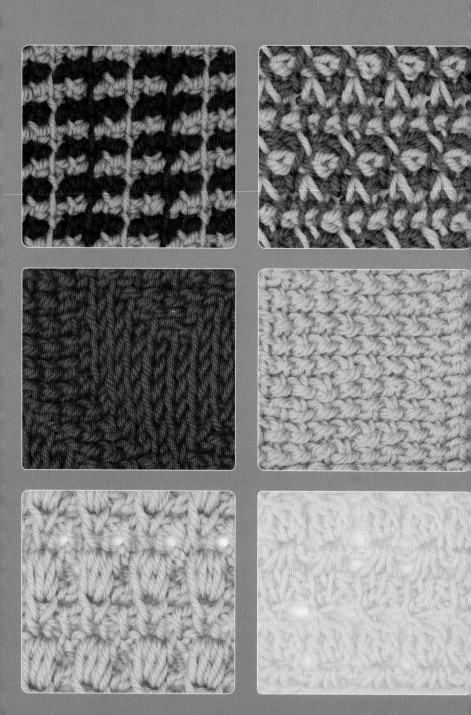

Close-up photos and step-by-step directions
for the all-important Foundation Row
and the basic stitches of Tunisian Crochet.

General Instructions

This handy reference guide is filled
with photos and explanations that
you will use again and again as
you learn to make the 61 pattern
stitches in this book. You'll learn
where to work in the starting chain
to create the Foundation Row, and
you'll have directions for all the basic
stitches -- together in one place for
your convenience. There also are
instructions for decreasing
and for changing colors.

ABBREVIATIONS

ch(s)	chain(s)	tfs	Tunisian Full Stitch
cm	centimeters	tks	Tunisian Knit Stitch
mm	millimeters	tps	Tunisian Purl Stitch
tbs	Tunisian Bobble Stitch	trs	Tunisian Reverse Stitch
tds	Tunisian Double Stitch	tss	Tunisian Simple Stitch
tds2tog	Tunisian Double Stitch 2 together	tss2tog	Tunisian Simple Stitch 2 together
tes	Tunisian Extended Stitch	YO	yarn over

Yarn Weight Symbol & Names	LACE 0	SUPER FINE 1	FINE 2	LIGHT 3	MEDIUM 4	BULKY 5	SUPER BULKY 6
Type of Yarns in Category	Fingering, 10-count crochet thread	Sock, Fingering Baby	Sport, Baby	DK, Light Worsted	Worsted, Afghan, Aran	Chunky, Craft, Rug	Bulky, Roving
Crochet Gauge* Ranges in Single Crochet to 4" (10 cm)	32-42 double crochets**	21-32 sts	16-20 sts	12-17 sts	11-14 sts	8-11 sts	5-9 sts
Advised Hook Size Range	Steel*** 6,7,8 Regular hook B-1	B-1 to E-4	E-4 to 7	7 to I-9	I-9 to K-10.5	K-10.5 to M-13	M-13 and larger

*GUIDELINES ONLY: The chart above reflects the most commonly used gauges and hook sizes for specific yarn categories.

◼☐☐☐ **BEGINNER**	Projects for first-time crocheters using basic stitches. Minimal shaping.
◼◼☐☐ **EASY**	Projects using yarn with basic stitches, repetitive stitch patterns, simple color changes, and simple shaping and finishing.
◼◼◼☐ **INTERMEDIATE**	Projects using a variety of techniques, such as basic lace patterns or color patterns, mid-level shaping and finishing.
◼◼◼◼ **EXPERIENCED**	Projects with intricate stitch patterns, techniques and dimension, such as non-repeating patterns, multi-color techniques, fine threads, small hooks, detailed shaping and refined finishing.

CROCHET HOOKS															
U.S.	B-1	C-2	D-3	E-4	F-5	G-6	H-8	I-9	J-10	K-10½	L-11	M/N-13	N/P-15	P/Q	Q	S
Metric - mm	2.25	2.75	3.25	3.5	3.75	4	5	5.5	6	6.5	8	9	10	15	16	19

CROCHET TERMINOLOGY	
UNITED STATES	INTERNATIONAL
slip stitch (slip st) =	single crochet (sc)
single crochet (sc) =	double crochet (dc)
half double crochet (hdc) =	half treble crochet (htr)
double crochet (dc) =	treble crochet(tr)
treble crochet (tr) =	double treble crochet (dtr)
double treble crochet (dtr) =	triple treble crochet (ttr)
triple treble crochet (tr tr) =	quadruple treble crochet (qtr)
skip =	miss

SYMBOLS & TERMS

★ — work instructions following ★ as many **more** times as indicated in addition to the first time.

( ) or [ ] — work enclosed instructions **as many** times as specified by the number immediately following **or** work all enclosed instructions in the stitch or space indicated **or** contains explanatory remarks.

colon (:) — the number(s) given after a colon at the end of a row denote(s) the number of stitches you should have on that row.

TUNISIAN CROCHET

Each row in Tunisian crochet is a two-step process.

The first step (Forward Pass) will pull up loops and leave them on the hook. The second step (Return Pass) will work the loops off the hook until one loop remains. This loop is the first stitch of the next row.

FOUNDATION ROW

Chain the number indicated in the pattern stitch.

Forward Pass: Pull up a loop in horizontal bar of second ch from hook and each ch across *(Fig. 1a)*.

To close (Return Pass): YO and draw through one loop on hook **(ch 1 made)** *(Fig. 1b)*, (YO and draw through 2 loops on hook) across *(Fig. 1c)*: one loop.

Fig. 1a

Fig. 1b

Fig. 1c

TUNISIAN SIMPLE STITCH
(abbreviated tss)

Insert hook from **right** to **left** under next vertical bar *(Fig. 2)*, YO and pull up a loop.

Fig. 2

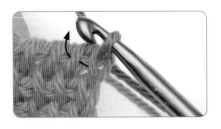

TUNISIAN KNIT STITCH
(abbreviated tks)

Insert hook from **front** to **back** between front and back vertical bars of next st *(Fig. 3)*, YO and pull up a loop.

Fig. 3

TUNISIAN KNIT STITCH PURLED

With yarn in **front** of work, insert hook from **front** to **back** between front and back vertical bars of next st *(Fig. 4)*, YO and pull up a loop.

Fig. 4

TUNISIAN REVERSE STITCH
(abbreviated trs)

With hook at **back** of work, insert hook from **right** to **left** under **back** of next vertical bar *(Fig. 5)*, YO and pull up a loop.

Fig. 5

TUNISIAN PURL STITCH
(abbreviated tps)

With yarn in **front** of work, insert hook from **right** to **left** under next vertical bar *(Fig. 6)*, YO and pull up a loop.

Fig. 6

TUNISIAN TWISTED KNIT STITCH

Using the hook tip, pull the front vertical bar over until you see the back vertical bar *(Fig. 7)*. Insert hook between vertical bars, YO and pull up a loop.

Fig. 7

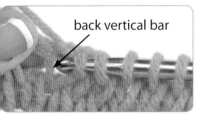

back vertical bar

TUNISIAN TWISTED SIMPLE STITCH

Using the hook tip, grasp the front vertical bar of next st, twist the hook down and around, forming a twist *(Fig. 8)*, YO and pull up a loop.

Fig. 8

TUNISIAN EXTENDED STITCH *(abbreviated tes)*

Insert hook from **front** to **back** between front and back vertical bars of next st, YO and pull up a loop, [YO *(Fig. 9)* and draw through one loop on hook **(chain 1 made)**].

Fig. 9

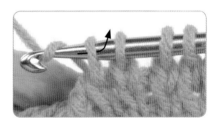

TUNISIAN DOUBLE STITCH
(abbreviated tds)

YO, insert hook from **right** to **left** under next vertical bar, YO and pull up a loop, YO and draw through 2 loops on hook *(Figs. 10a & b)*.

Fig. 10a

Fig. 10b

TUNISIAN BOBBLE STITCH
(abbreviated tbs)

Work 3 tds in stitch indicated *(Fig. 11a)*, YO and draw through 3 loops *(Fig. 11b)*.

Fig. 11a

Fig. 11b

TUNISIAN CROSSED STITCH (uses 2 sts)

Skip next vertical bar, insert hook from **right** to **left** under next vertical bar *(Fig. 12a)*, YO and pull up a loop, insert hook from **right** to **left** under skipped vertical bar, YO and pull up a loop *(Fig. 12b)*.

Fig. 12a

Fig. 12b

TUNISIAN DOUBLE CROSSED STITCH

(uses 3 sts)

Skip next 2 vertical bars, work tds under next vertical bar *(Fig. 13a)*, work tds under first skipped vertical bar *(Fig. 13b)*.

Fig. 13a

Fig. 13b

TUNISIAN FULL STITCH

(abbreviated tfs)

Insert hook from **front** to **back** under horizontal bar between two sts *(Fig. 14)*, YO and pull up a loop.

Fig. 14

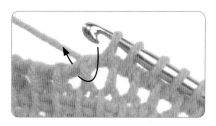

TUNISIAN SLIP STITCH

Insert hook from **right** to **left** under next vertical bar *(Fig. 15)* and leave loop on hook.

Fig. 15

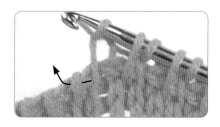

DECREASES

TUNISIAN DOUBLE STITCH 2 TOGETHER
(abbreviated tds2tog)

YO, insert hook from **right** to **left** under next 2 vertical bars *(Fig. 16)*, YO and pull up a loop, YO and draw through 2 loops on hook.

Fig. 16

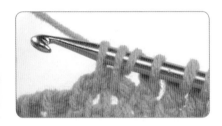

TUNISIAN SIMPLE STITCH 2 TOGETHER *(abbreviated tss2tog)*

Insert hook from **right** to **left** under next 2 vertical bars *(Fig. 17a)*, YO and draw through 2 loops on hook *(Fig. 17b)*.

Fig. 17a

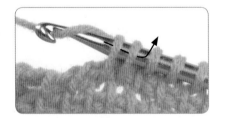

Fig. 17b

CHANGING COLORS

To change colors on a return pass, close across to last 2 sts. Drop the old yarn and with the new yarn *(Fig. 18a)*, yarn over and draw through 2 loops on hook.

Fig. 18a

To change colors on a forward pass, work across all sts. Drop the old yarn, yarn over and pull through one loop *(Fig. 18b)*, then close with the new yarn.

Fig. 18b